# Being Many Seeds

# Being    Many    Seeds

Marilyn McCabe

GRAYSON BOOKS
West Hartford, CT
www.graysonbooks.com

Being Many Seeds
Copyright © Marilyn McCabe
Published by Grayson Books
West Hartford, Connecticut

ISBN: 978-1-7335568-1-1

Book & cover design by Cindy Stewart
Cover art © Nina Shengold

# Acknowledgments

"As stars are not" in *Sonic Boom*, under the title "We Are All Strangers Here."

"Wind attracts wind" in *Amethyst Review*, as "The Unfolding Earth."

Afternoon steeped into two cups.
He tells of a tree gone wife,
how bitter the weather.
The winter long silence.
Exile blooms in him.
A table's grain fades
as a story written in earth.

::

        steeped
He tells
how bitter
The winter
Exile blooms     him

               in earth

::

how bitter

    blooms

                earth

*Pierre Teilhard de Chardin, Jesuit priest and scientist, believed in God and? but? studied the bones of prehistoric humankind like Peking Man, reading the bones of the old stone maker, the world in his hands. War was coming. What could he make of this?*

A young man in black pedals a black bike holds
a black umbrella light rain plunks everything
greening around him and pink
magnolia lets loose a petal high
crow transects his route the pedaler
glimpsing it all upside down in puddle
even as he rolls away


::

   young
              light
greening


                          in puddle
        rolls away

::

              light
greening


                away


*Teilhard believed that a system cannot be understood outside of time: all things are in process; nothing is static. We each are systems in the process of becoming, even as we are part of a larger system which also is unfolding.*

Tongue wakes to speak
morning before my eyes
and stumbles over some name
sought and forgotten.
This seems to be true:
Tasting is the essence
of being awake,
and as it is a sense not retained
well in memory, days are
for sampling flights
of what the waking makes.

::

Tongue wakes
morning
and stumbles


Tasting
   being
and

    sampling
        the waking

::


   be



    the waking


*But can systems learn from their own mistakes? Evolution would lead us to believe, to some degree, yes. Teilhard felt hopeful: that sense of emergence and possibility.*

As stars are not
the mystic harbor of my wishes
nor mass but space and burning,
so are my questions.

I come to every strange city
as a refugee coming home,
the old streets as if new,
a familiar portico, flourished pedestal,

view from this dusty window.
I am this name unasked.


::

    stars are

                      burning
          questions

I come to every       city

          as if
a

          dusty window

::

    stars are

                      burning

        every    city


*Teilhard de Chardin wandered into the realm of physics, considered the molecule's ascension toward the cell, the cell's journey toward the creation of conscious beings, and he compared the evolutionary trip of the physical and that of the spirit.*

You are moving toward faster things
as evening blows papers around your step,
the hum of sidewalks pale and pocked;
you remove your hat with flourish at the red light.
You have told your stories,
striding corridors of skyscrapers, which reach
farther from you and you walk faster
following the breeze. Horns blow, echo
clank of subway cover over
and over. You are turning, step assured, kicking
aside the breeze. Ah, you are
finished business, in no need of direction,
but still not
faster than the night.

::

   evening blows

               your hat with
                   stories

                             which
                                echo
                 over
and over
                 you are
             in   need of

       the night

::

                 you are

       the night

*Teilhard was born in the Auvergne, a sparsely populated area of ancient volcanoes, wild valleys, werewolf tales, and old languages. One could believe almost anything there.*

While the day is its own
autocracy, I am citizen
staring out at world,
touch the cool glass of rain's
mirror. Color deepens
then fades, a slow flicker
as if I am blinking,
as I must open the eyes
inside myself to keep
democracy alive.

::

    the day is

        world
  the cool glass of
  Color
      a    flicker
    blinking
        the eyes
      to keep
    alive

::

  the

      world

        the eyes
        keep
    alive


*He got the science wrong, according to the scientists, but it seemed Teilhard was on to something with regard to the evolution of culture and social structure. Evolution seems to favor the cooperative group. Certainly ants have taken over my backyard.*

Crosshatched hemlocks and rattlesnake
fern block the path.
I have entered the sunlit pasture.
In this clearing, shadows
stream toward clouds,
clasp at a cliff fissure.

::

        hemlocks and

I

stream
toward clouds
clasp   a cliff

::

        hemlocks and

I

clasp

*Teilhard asserted that just as a cell cannot be well understood outside of its organism, humanity cannot be understood apart from the larger system within which we are a part, the cosmos. We are our own selves, but? and? we are a part of the system of each other, the earth, and the heavens.*

Crests and breaks, the land;
the trail and I surf it,
now on the edge, now under curl,
and we slide out into its wake,
rise and fall again.
I want to talk about time.
Further north and higher up,
among the stiff and brittle pines,
with moss the color of olive,
the sky martini-clear. Geologic time
in this approaching happy hour,
I'd like to sip this
until we're gone.

::

                the land

  on the edge

      again
I want to talk about


     this approaching     hour
I'd like to sip
until     gone

::

                the land

       approaching

    gone

*Teilhard asserted that just as a cell cannot be well understood outside of its organism, humanity cannot be understood apart from the larger system within which we are a part, the cosmos. We are our own selves, but? and? we are a part of the system of each other, the earth, and the heavens.*

Warm day, dusty, the bushes sere and lit with stars
of broken glass underneath.
We are shepherded into the antechamber, then sealed
against the outside air, harmful
to the ancient chemistry. Silence falls, and the inner door opens.
We dirty travelers shuffle forward,
holding our breath. We have only a short time together
under this dazzling pretend heaven.

::

    day                          lit with stars
broken

                          falls, and
We    travelers shuffle
                                      together
       dazzling    heaven

::

                                   stars
                        and
We    travelers shuffle

                                together

*He asserted that cultures are subject to evolution, and that humanity is evolving toward greater interdependence, toward larger social units working in collaboration. I think of Eric Whitacre's virtual choir -- people from around the world singing into their computers, moshed together into a synchronized performance and shown with tiny portraits of all the participants, from a living room in New Delhi to a music studio in Taiwan to a bedroom in Sheboygan.*

A structure myself, I am holey,
barely discernible, as a toothpick tower.
(Would I were a reed through which wind passes.)
But I will tangle. I will think I'm something else.
I stomp around in world as god.
Empty largely, I am disturbance.
Ants too think they are large.
Grass casts its eyes skyward.
Space itself insensate, we beings
forget we're light.

::

          I am
          a
                     wind

                god
   ,   disturbance

   its   skyward

  light

::

          I am




    light

*I think of how radio programs cross the globe, now not only across airways but also across the internet, so when I'm laughing to Car Talk, you may be too, whoever you are, wherever you are, even though Tommy's been dead now three years. I think too of terrorist cells operating around the world in communication with each other. Of the global nature of hatred. What if it's not the best of us that's evolving, but the worst?*

Wind attracts wind,
sound comes along,
with seeds and a different dirt,
as the sea drags anything loose,
plants it where it has never belonged,
strange slate, a plant desperate for land.
Life wants itself. Will pay any price.
Are we the only species that mulls the past
incessantly, invest futures of jewels and virgins,
of heavenly hosts singing
beyond this land under our terrible feet?
We're dying to get there, love.

::

Wind

       and
  the sea

            desperate for land
        Will

incessantly invest      jewels and
   heavenly     singing

         , love

::

             land

incessantly

      singing

       love

*For Teilhard, the evolution of the grand system of which we are a part is intertwined with the evolution of humanity and our coming-together of intention and will. He believes that all this evolution has at its center, as its center-based force, centrifugal, God. I cannot make that leap with him.*

The old gods have flickered. Only smoke and kneelers
reveal where they were. How loud the intercession.
Reluctant to arrive, I turn away confirmed.
They were never what I had hoped
they would be. A chaos of prayers has collided.
Can I close my ears to the scattered amen?

::

    old gods

                were       loud

                     I had hoped

they would be

        my ears

::

    old gods



                        hoped

they would be

        my ears

*And? But? what if he's wrong—that a system's impetus is not to continue itself through betterment?*

*Or what if in the process of the cosmic system's emergence, we humankind, like a tail, like an extra toe, are what becomes edited out?*

So much grows here. I have been
a tree in this oasis. I am only one
in a world, and that through silence.
Want and halt is here and also large wonder.
Life whirls lived, from a shivering palm frond,
from the wind, and sudden thunder,
from the orange's woven aroma, and many long
vines. From the warm beat, going away, of the bird wing.
All these things as seeds in the ground.
In growing, roots bracket, entangle,
trunks increase and in treetops an afterglow
in which I become myself evening.

::

                I have been

a
                                wonder
      lived    shivering
from the wind

                and many

        seeds
  growing

::

                I have been

                      many

        seeds

*But I don't want to leave you like this, Teilhard, with all this distance between us. Let us say I have heard you. Let us say we have connected as sinews in the cosmic body. Let us say we have, however briefly, been moving the bones. Let us say we have briefly been.*

# About the Author

Marilyn McCabe's work has garnered her an Orlando Prize from A Room of Her Own Foundation, the Hilary Tham Capital Collection contest award from The Word Works, resulting in publication of her book of poems *Perpetual Motion*, and two artist grants from the New York State Council on the Arts. Her second book of poems, *Glass Factory*, was published in 2016. Her poems and videopoetry have been published in a variety of print and online literary magazines. She blogs about writing and reading at Owrite:marilynonaroll.wordpress.com.

www.ingramcontent.com/pod-product-compliance
Lightning Source LLC
Chambersburg PA
CBHW070120110526
44587CB00016BA/2744